A SPEAKER IS A WILDERNESS

A SPEAKER IS A WILDERNESS

POEMS ON THE SACRED PATH
FROM BROKEN TO WHOLE

ANNA GOODMAN HERRICK

Monkfish Book Publishing Company
Rhinebeck, New York

Paperback ISBN 978-1-958972-37-3
eBook ISBN 978-1-958972-38-0

Library of Congress Cataloging-in-Publication Data

Names: Herrick, Anna Goodman, author.
Title: A speaker is a wilderness : poems on the sacred path from broken to whole / Anna Goodman Herrick.
Description: Rhinebeck, New York : Monkfish Book Publishing Company, 2024.
Identifiers: LCCN 2023045142 (print) | LCCN 2023045143 (ebook) | ISBN 9781958972373 (paperback) | ISBN 9781958972380 (ebook)
Subjects: LCGFT: Poetry.
Classification: LCC PS3608.E7737 S64 2024 (print) | LCC PS3608.E7737 (ebook) | DDC 811/.6--dc23/eng/20240111
LC record available at https://lccn.loc.gov/2023045142
LC ebook record available at https://lccn.loc.gov/2023045143

Book and cover design by Colin Rolfe

Monkfish Book Publishing Company
22 East Market Street, Suite 304
Rhinebeck, New York 12572
(845) 876-4861
monkfishpublishing.com

In memory of
צפורה מלכה בת פנינה ז״ל
Tzipporah Malka, Z"L

HOW TO BLESS YOURSELF

If you are waiting for a spiritual leader to tell you,

write what you need to hear

and read it back to yourself and call it blessing.

Call the act of doing this a blessing.

Call yourself a blessing.

CONTENTS

PRAYER FOR RAIN

A human being is in the likeness of a small world.
— Ibn Ezra (circa 11th – 12th century c.e.)

Tell me what a world looks like: how big its hands are,
how much it can hold.

Pray, my mother whispers. She holds her own hands
together and my father clasps his.

We sit alone, the three of us,
in the closed off hospital waiting room
that stores people away
from the folks with hope.

I know my brother is already dead.
I had not lived 7 years.

adam olam katan
a person is a small world,
        a microcosm of the universe

*

What is that sound?
I ask my mother, in her bed
beside her. The screech of geese,
the low call of cows at dusk, the moan
of a blue whale. *That's your father*
crying. The ecosphere has new sounds now,
lower, higher, louder—
pitch expands its reach
in all directions.

adam olam katan
a person is a small world,
        a microcosm of the universe,
        a tiny forever

*

This is hard for them, a woman's mouth
informs me, her face
peering down at mine. I wander my home and watch
strangers hug my parents.

*

A child is his parents' whole world,
my best friend, cross-legged on my bed,
shakes her head, weary, emulating
a stranger in the living room.
Now their world is gone. I am also a child
of his parents.

*

My parents said something must be wrong
with you, you didn't cry at your brother's funeral. I think,
something is wrong with me: my brother
is dead. I turn away and wait for the school bus.

The creation of the world was like the creation of humanity,
for everything that HaKadosh Baruch Hu, the Holy Blessed One,
created in the world, the Holy Blessed One created in the human being.
— Otzar Midrashim, Agadat Olam Katan

*

A child's closet encompasses a biosphere:
Halloween candy hidden and stockpiled,
a kid can stay in here and live
on melted and stale bite-size Snickers. I am sure
the world could not hold
one more person crying in public,
out loud. My parents are my world.

I sit on the floor,
against the closed closet door. From above me,
the flannels and denims caress

my face. I feel something
wet on my cheeks, droplets of warm rain
from my eyes. Something will grow here.

DIASPORA PRAYER OF THE REFUGEE'S GRANDCHILD

I know how to wrap my hair in a scarf, black and abloom
with fuchsias and call myself my own grandmother.

I know there are a thousand names for G-d
bound around tongues

and a thousand ways to say my name
in all the languages I have longed for, from the
places I have tried to call home.

I know I am a guest unsought in a stolen
guest house and the refugee

who lives on in my blood took shelter
built from an occupier's dream of home. I know
this is not a prayer to be spoken lightly.

I know my frame remains a visitor, provisional
and the God alive in my body took shelter
built from an ad exec's imagination of a woman

and this Limitless is demolishing
and rebuilding her. I know when the Sacred
asks her to leave, she will have to listen. I know
when the Sacred asks her to leave she will have to listen.

I know I am already an ancestor and it's time
to act accordingly. Somewhere, the future
is remembering me.

TENDING SEGULAH

May that pit in your stomach
be a seed. May the heaviness
in your chest signal the roots
pushing through.
May something
nourishing
germinate
from you,
from this
moment.
Emerge,
nourish,
root,
seed.

BOTTLENECKED

In the basement, the boy's home's underworld,
I hyped my hungry
and empty belly, my bone-torso
emaciated in my training
bra: I would fit through that doggy door
of the target house the best. I could shove
my way in, take and leave
even better than a boy.

And each boy ignored my campaign, left
me waiting alone in the Mourning Fields of broken
furniture, in a junkyard womb,
slumped on the couch like a boy, faded
cushions slack beneath me, for their return, someboy
else's parents screaming at each other
above my head, their stomping and crashing
that wine-face-sea, all of us in search of home—
each of us flailing our arms, gasping, *Here*—
a house of off-brand Calypsos, begging
every shipwrecked visitor who passes by
to stay.

In the above-world, the boys played watch guard
on a shadowy lawn
so one boy could enter and take what he wanted
from a woman's home
he'd been invited into (aren't they all like that–)
a woman welcoming a boy mowing her grass
in for water, the boy watching
the room, wondering how he'll get back in, tracking
her animal's path.

The next morning, I take my seat atop
the cafeteria table and tell
the girls it was me who swam through
that pet flap last night,
into the stranger's house, grabbed and dragged
the bag of bottles back to the basement.

Look at me, how I guzzled the red river Lethe, swelled
into the Goddess of Oblivion.
My body was good for something.

I steal the story
even as the girls call me criminal,
the first among us, my throat filled
with shame, because being a thief is better
than being nothing.

Intruding
like a boy
is better
than being left and forgotten
like a girl.

What else these girls don't know:

Last night, the boys
couldn't even boy right,
as busted as I couldn't girl. These trial-
size men had come back
to the basement, hands shaking,
as if they knew for a moment
their bodies were made for more possibility,
dropped all the bottles,
smashing open a blood-red flood
across the floor, libations for all
the dead trying to reach
each of us
and let us know something good
will happen
when we're not
                           so, so small.

TENDER AND WILD,

like my mother:
Earth. Within me, the storm,
the wreckage,
whole communities sprout up
to find each other, make ceremony
for our dead, nurse the gasping

back to life. New houses are built
in me. Protests.
Whole uprisings. I am made
of multitudes
that cannot be contained.

THEOPRAXIS OF A TWELVE-YEAR-OLD GIRL IN THE SUBURBS

asked to be apathetic and ruthless,
become
the catacomb
naked
sinner
moving

which is the only way you knew
to child,

a thunder
stumbling
below
slender
trash is also made
in an image
make yourself
a strong girl
in the past
tense,

to that basement
of inequity and

heroes of the wayward struggle

for pleasure
delinquents
degenerate
shadow crusade

our stomping a thunder
our stumbling and crashing איכה *ayeka*—
G-d rumbling inside us, asking
our newly formed selves, *where are you?*

children naked in closets whispering,
show me something I can grab onto

HYMN TO BLOODLETTING, SACRIFICE OF BECOMING

How did you come to grow
ancient and stubborn inside me,
catastrophic like the moon?
When they call the uterus home
of hysteria, believe them.

Watch them draw fire
against the living of our ruckus,
how they come for us—

You, cycloptic bloodshot, red-eyed with rage,
when they hold you accountable
for all time and every pleasure and harm,
while they take you by force,
inside your own cave,

Watch
how they make you a god,
how they try to tame you like a beast
because they don't know
how to make a home in either—
the holy
or the animal
of you.

ROUGH BARK

this is not a poem about a virus. this is a poem about the sunlight trembling in through the curtains. this is not a poem about dying. this is a poem about the willows shimmying and the time v told me, *you'll know you're where you need to be when you can see the trees smile* and I watched and waited and then I could. this is not a poem about my lungs hurting. this is about roots squishing into the juicy ground. i'm not going to talk about coughing

in this verse. this line is not about k on a ventilator, it's about epiphytes, plants that live on other plants but are not parasitic, so this is about orchids growing on avocado trees. this is not about n staggering away from the hospital, calling to tell us there's no medicine for her, that all she can do is go home. this is about how upland orchids do best in partial shade and how avocado trees boast rough bark well-suited to root-attachment. this is not about z washing r's body himself, before carrying him into the ground. this is about how you must water or mist the orchid roots daily if you want them to attach to the tree. they are so exposed, no longer resting in soil, not yet reoriented. this is not about d laying cuttings from l's garden onto his shrouded body. this is not about how, when honoring both a person and their privacy, a name becomes unspeakable, like g-d. this is not a poem for the dead. this is a poem for the living. but if the dead want to join in, they are invited. i'm not going to say kaddish

in this one, but if i did, i might remind myself that in the mourner's kaddish, there is no mention of death. i might remember that with proper care, a land-bound plant separated from the soil can adapt to living in this new way.

CALL ME BY MY HEALING NAME

1.

I thought lipstick was a missile
a woman launched into the stratosphere

and chose who to rescue in her arms
and who to leave

blown open in her wake. I thought eyeliner
was a prophet

delineating the parameters
of a holy war.

My age was the age a boy
becomes answerable for his actions

and his father no longer
accountable for his sins. I am one year late

to assert myself a woman
because I am afraid

to sing.

2.

At thirteen, I bear as many years to my body as moons
in a *Shanah Me'uberet,* a year swelling
with possibility, with a thirteenth moon, the good

luck moon. Chances to sanctify
new moons bursting
with blessings. Ari's mother danced naked

under the new moon when
the neighbors saw and,
in a New England winter, convicted

her of witchcraft. And I don't yet know
she was carrying on
her ancestral promise— only that no one will

sit next to her son at lunch. When he and I match
our left eyes to Clockwork
Orange, neighbors whisper. When he slow-dances

his wrist against a blade that year,
I overhear a mother warn her children
his mother's a witch. Her husband agrees, blames

Ari's eyeliner his mother lets him wear. No one blames
their concrete blame tied to his feet
as he tries to swim upstream.

3.

I praise Ari's mother for her wild
and Chaya cautions
me against witchcraft.

In Chaya's basement, we call each other
by our Hebrew names. Our names we give
in public disappear. We go

underground. At thirteen, my age holds a year
for each child of Ya'akov who is named,
counting the daughter

דִּינָה בַּת־לֵאָה
Dinah Daughter-of-Leah,

and nowhere in her story does it say
she is called this way because
this is her healing name, because to say,

a name, then child-of-her-mother's name
is how we pray
for healing

and she will need healing

but she is called this way
because this is her healing name, because she will need healing

so let's say it here.

And what was done to her, says the Torah,
such ought not to be done.

At thirteen, my age holds a year for each of these children
of Ya'akov, a year for each known child born

to the One Who Wrestles G-d,
and so who G-d renames.

4.

I dye my hair violet, the spectrum
almost out of breath, cut it all off
and leave it course. When the dye runs

out, I let girls try out colors
in my hair. I am technicolor
and some days shame.

At thirteen, I have lived as many years
as the Rambam's principals of faith.
I am the final principal, that we will be resurrected,

though I am unclear how. I have lived as many years
as there are Divine Attributes of Mercy
governing the world. My name I reserve

for basements, the name of
the woman who taught us how to pray,
draws from one attribute: *Chanun*. Often translated as *grace*,

it means *to camp, to bend down*, as in
when *something great bends down
in kindness to someone small.*

5.

I can't find my body.

I hope my army surplus green pants
and white tank top will camouflage
what heaves underneath.

In class, Joey drops
a pencil and tells me to pick it up
so he can look down my shirt.

I want my body back.

6.

I pray my dog tags will help
my missing brigade of angels find me
in the wilderness

and bring my body home. I draw wings on the inside
of my knee-high steel-toe black leather boots.

7.

My mother tells me when she was my age
Your mama wears army boots
was an insult. I am a your mama joke to my mother.

I am, increasingly, my own mother. My mother wears army boots.

8.

My father tells me he fears my close-cropped hair
is his fault and hopes I kiss men soon. Gather in.

Rachel with the long blue hair tells me she likes girls.
I write her a love letter. Jenny tells me Rachel told her

about the letter and asks me was it a love letter
and I tell her no so she tells Rachel no.

9.

When I march across the football field, in my white army
undershirt tank, to try out for the cheerleading team

because I will never give up on a good costume
I don't know I am on battle ground until the players charge

towards me making dog noises and whistling. Katherine unties
her sweater from her waist. *Put it on so they stop.*

Let them whistle. I am the perfect age for a holy war.
I am the children's war.

No one knows a good war like a 13-year-old.

10.

No I don't know how I wound up in the woods
that year holding
still under a hot sun facing

X asking me if I remember what he did
but I remember
I remembered what he did

and told him I did not.
He tells me if I do, don't tell
anyone. I have seen this exchange

on a school video where the host instructs,
tell someone anyway. But I don't. I remember not giving up
his name as if to protect myself,

sure I would be safer telling no one
than if I danced in public
under a new moon.

I would be blamed by everyone. Some days
I will wonder if that many people would be right
and blame myself.

I remember not giving up what happened
to not give up anything more
of myself. It was too humiliating to acknowledge

I had lost my body and I didn't know
how to get it back.

It was too humiliating to admit
I was awake inside this body. I was here.

11.

One story goes that Dinah Daughter-of-Leah *went out*
and a girl must never— and so she was punished
with the assault against her—

BUT WHAT WAS DONE TO HER, SUCH OUGHT NOT TO BE DONE.

And the real story goes that Dinah went out,
that she was outgoing,
because she was brave.

Like her mother.

And concerning her, they devise the proverb: Like mother like daughter.

12.

Thirteen: I am the number of years old
as there are days
of yom tovs, good days, festival days,
celebrations, in a year

in diaspora.

I am scattered, dispersed,

and ripe
for celebrating. Gather in,
from all corners of the Earth,
to the holiest land, your body.

13.

Can I go back in time? Can I find
what ripped and mend it? If you are still
stuck there, little one, I found you

this:

Rise up on the tips of the toes in the direction of the moon
while reciting three times:

As I dance toward you,
but cannot touch you,
so shall all my evil-intended enemies be unable
to touch me.

and this:

אַז מען בענשט ראָש חוֹדֶשׁ זאָגט מען דאָס
Az men bensht rash khudsh zagt men dos
When one blesses the New Moon one says this:

Look down, look from heaven upon your holy congregation who stand
and pray. Their hearts are
broken. They rage and roar and are not silent.

NOTES

"And concerning her... like daughter." is from Babylonian Talmud (Gen. Rabbah 80:1)

"Rise up on… cannot touch me" is from the Kiddush Levanah (Sanctification of the Moon), a traditional Jewish ritual.

"When one blessses…. silent" is from *Prayer for Blessing the New Moon on the Shabbat Mevorkhim*, credited to Sarah bat Tovim (AKA Soreh Bas Toyvim) (ca. 17th c.), from *Tkhine of Three Gates*, Compiled and Translation from Yiddish by Tracy Guren Klirs, Ida Cohen Selavan, and Gella Schweid Fishman in *The Merit of Our Mothers: A Bilingual Anthology of Jewish Women's Prayers* (University of Pittsburgh Press/ HUC Press, 1992)

THE POETRY CRITIC SAYS DON'T WRITE ABOUT
THE MOON

And I know the moon
is perfect. And we're so cruel
to perfect things.

BAMIDBAR
במדבר

I didn't want a priest. I wanted what we all want
in the wilderness after losing our home:
to find a place to wash.

I wanted the daybreak's womb of mercy
to birth me new and clean
my grubby fingers over the copper basin

within the pitcher's pour. If there was a ritual
my ancients might have done, I wanted to re-
member its limbs

to my communal body, implant its rhizome
throughout my red earth. I wanted
to dip my bitter

spine in saltwater and sing to the sea its name:
Alive. I wanted to know something holy
and present could dwell here

and adorn her with ornaments– the nose ring,
the amulet, the veil– study sacred text with her
throughout one night, and on another fall asleep and stir

like a lion, in that alley between
the dusk sky's first three stars and the dawn,
to roar over our exile from each other.

מדבר מדבר
m/d/b/r m/d/b/r
wilderness speaks
a speaker is a wilderness

I wanted

G-d. I wanted G-d. I wanted to know
where I came from and a *tzadik* to trace the map
of my breath and say *here.*

LOVE LETTER TO MY WORRIES FROM INSIDE THIS BODY

I want to tell you
about the waves and the sunlight,
how the wind sounds
like the ocean in the desert,
how all things return
in new forms—
the broken bottle

as soft, translucent gems. I want to promise
you that all the garbage you toss
will find its way back
to someone and you can
experience the sun set in the east
on an island. Sometimes, it's worth the solitude,
other times you'll find nearby islands, and learn
alone is a word that shapeshifts.

We can come home
to ourselves
and belong—
and the meaning of *ourselves* stretches
and contracts, holds
as many and as few people as we can
and *can*
can swell

and break, ebb and breathe.
I want you to remember
we belong

to each other
and to the ocean
and to the ocean that dwells inside us—
we, too, are the universe,
expanding, in love, embracing
so much grief
and joy.

THE OFFERING

He wasn't much for giving gifts
or for speaking. He looked confused
when we spoke of presents: *Isn't being alive*
enough for you? My grandfather Leiby, tall

as the Babel Tower, the ghosts living inside him
long since dispersed, conversing in Hungarian, Yiddish,
Hebrew, English, and fear, never asked
what I wanted. Never scoured the streets, searching

for the perfect tribute to anyone or offered
a box and watched with glimmering eyes
someone tear off shiny paper. But one afternoon,
after Alzheimer's and Parkinson's tightened their ribbons

around him, his shaking hands rummaged through
his tool closet in the apartment hallway, swatting away
his family imploring him to sit down. He staggered
towards the kitchen table, cradling a mountain

of pencil stubs and lay them down,
over the floral oilcloth. He must have been rescuing these
all his life. He pushed them towards me
and showed how he had found space left to sharpen

each stub. *Here*, he offered me:
the almost finished,
the used up,
the nearly irredeemable
like us
too have a chance.

FOR A MOMENT

Forget the idea you have
a past. Forget remembering
the expectations you had
for your life. Forget
disappointment. Sit with me
where unfinished wood
and steel nails become
this small table.
Let's pretend this iron teapot
is the heaviest thing
we have carried.

GENIZAH

*genizah - a storage place where worn out ritual objects and unusable
sacred texts, especially texts that name God, are held, to keep them safe
before they are buried*

how many times have I cried out, *God*
and more polite people would have called
it in vain?

what of each of us is a genizah?

Tanna'it Asnat Barzani held the Secret Name
in her mouth and when she opened it, doves flew out
of the burning
synagogue— or was it angels? angels that looked like doves—
and what are angels?

Rebbe Leibeleh learned 3 things in Kotzk.
1. We are not angels. 2. We can become greater than angels. 3.—

I am catching my breath/ on our tongues,
words have caught/ fire. Here are the doves: *hallelu—*
buried in a Yiddish lullaby   *hi-lalulu lulu lulu*   a niggun/ for
a baby

You must know the words to say them.

praise yah   praise yah   praise—

    gevurah-din: *chesed:*
if you believe you can ruin,   *believe you can repair*

tiferet:
גנ   גניזה
gan is in *genizah*
the garden hiding within
the storage for the used up

Avraham could see a portal to the Garden
in the cave so he buried
his beloved there.   O Sarah,
did you reproach the first *adam*
like the sages say the dying righteous must?

חִי   יָה
yah   ḥai
so close to mirror
images
made
        almost
        in each other

I am exhausted/ of blaming/ what is ruined/
in me

Everything names G-d.
Everything is usable.

NOTES

"If you believe you can ruin, believe you can repair" (Original: אם אתה מאמין,
שיכולין לקלקל, תאמין שיכולין לתקן) is from *Likutey Moharan*, Part II, Torah 112:1,
Rebbe Nachman of Breslov (translation A. Goodman Herrick)

FOR RICKY'S NYC, WHO LOVED ME WHEN

Ricky's NYC, 1989 - 2020

And for us, who congregated
at the counter, placing our faith
in this convenience store of dreams,

if what you dreamed of finding
was a pot of gold
glitter for your eyelids, to sample free
at midnight at 16 years old.

For us, who tried
on neon purple wigs in the mirror, just to imagine
affording them.

For us who dared to look
as the weathered club kids
admonished us, *close your eyes
and hold still,*
and affixed silver eyelashes
to our lids. For us for whom our young elders
revealed their crinkled singles
to the cashier and bestowed
these gifts upon us.

For us, who have loved the underworld
then disavowed
the underworld and never learned how to love
it properly until
the earth closed up—

For us who have known how the pomegranate
felt, dripping and juicy and sweet
and traded for girlhood
without our consent,

For us who have needed a club with a platform
to dance on in platform heels
where the ground isn't pulled out from under us—

I have gold lipstick in my medicine
cabinet and black nail polish
and glitter powder in every hue
and a drawer stocked
full with boxes of fake eyelashes,

and I still don't know how
to glue them on gracefully
on my own out here
but I will try with you
and I will ask nothing in return.

BUT WHAT IF GENERATIONAL TRAUMA *IS* GENERATIONAL WISDOM

I.

Are you going outside to be melancholy? Your mother
asks you as a preteen, your fingers wrapped
around the doorknob. You know now
she's been watching you.

It's a funny word, *melancholy*, and she has fun with it.
You smile back, nod, and leave.

It's a thing you do, disappear
from a group as they share laughter,
and walk out to the edge
of the street. Or on the day
your friends board the bus
to the theme park, you decide you
want to be home.

There is that afternoon in your early teens,
when you live on your own already
and your mother meets you in a café.

You confess you carry a sadness
and you don't know why. She tells you
about survival— your grandmother
in Auschwitz death camp with her sisters,
their parents murdered on their first day.

She tells you about Lilly,
your grandmother's little sister who fought a kapo
for a woman and her children to be spared.

She tells you about Lilly celebrating her own liberation
with her first taxi ride, from Sighet
to Bucharest, and being shot
dead on the way.

She tells you about looking for your grandmother's brother
after the war, *no, call it what it was, the murders, the genocide,*
finding out he was captured by Nazis,
then when liberation came,
he was mistaken for them, captured,
and imprisoned.

She tells you about fleeing—
great-grandmothers who ran
from pogroms in Odessa, and
places in Belarus she couldn't remember,
and from Sighet with a son
who became your grandfather. She tells you about
the woman who schlepped tradition on her back,

and couldn't find it anywhere in the man who'd paid
for her boat to America. She tells you about women

who buried themselves
in men who buried themselves
in factory jobs and who made your mother
practice hiding in a New York City apartment
for *when they come for us.*

She tells you about Talmud scholars of Romania
and great Rabbbis of Brooklyn
and their orphaned children
who loved you. She doesn't tell you about herself.
Maybe you know.

For a moment you can breathe. The sadness hovers
outside of you.

II.

You don't know you are making
your own sadness worth keeping
now— your own fleeing
from home. Your own terror

as you make your way alone,
your *yichus,*
your lineage.

You don't yet understand you can make something
else, something easier to hold. That your *yichus* includes nights
studying by candle light
and dancing with Torah scrolls.

Your geneolical records originate from
the town of *broken and whole,*
from *in exile and here.* From
Midnight Rectification on your knees
and pray the Morning Service,
from, *this is where you cry,*
and *this is where you bow.*

Your progeny can be named after
say this bracha, this blessing: may this be an action
of healing, for You heal
without charge.

You are in the in between time, still wrestling
with grace, not yet given a new name. You don't yet know
what you are mother to.

For years, you will forget that conversation
as a teen when your mother met you.

You will have found your own man to bury yourself alive in
and not yet know you are underground. You will call the pine box
making a home.

The sadness stirs,
sleeping in your arms,
waking to suckle, yawning, drifting
back into sleep. In slumber,
its eyelids flutter. What it imagines,
you don't know.

You cradle its clammy body,
listen to its breath
against your chest. It looks
just like you, you almost believe
it came from you. You almost
believe it's yours.

ANCESTORS

What if I told you:
We were separated at birth
from our ancestors. Their mother
tongue had words
for what could save you. How the holy contracted
right before birthing
everything.

You spoke English.
You learned to aim for the light.

Before the world was created,
it was so dark in the womb,
and you were
so warm.

[if your heart is broken let it keep breaking]

if your heart is broken let it keep breaking let it shatter
into a million pieces let it shard let it cut
you wide open you will never be the same
and sometimes this can be a good thing your tears
yes will salt your wounds for a while we have all
been torn open by each other let yourself come be the wound
opening you will embrace the world this way

LAMENTATIONS

We promised our children we didn't know
better. We were scared to say we knew
and chose worse. We could have protected them
from memories they believed they imagined,
the turn in their stomachs
they learned
not to trust. How great
was their *emunah*.

THE ROMANIAN JEW FLEES TO THE U.S. FOR A BETTER LIFE BUT ALL HER GRANDDAUGHTER DREAMS OF IS WAILING

*To the Last Professional Mourning Women of Romania
and My Grandmother Who, in their Absence, Wept Like a Professional*

We could leave this one-horse
cart hauling lumber to market and heave
over a coffin that cradles
a child and claim her:
our dead. We could cloak black wool scarves
around our heads and practice screaming
at my dinner table. We could visit graveyards
overrun with young clergy hushing us and dig
through our tattered songbooks
for dirges about the quiet
after your lover no longer whispers
secrets in your ear. We could shriek
into that silence then howl. Every week,
in a factory or an office, someone trades
in their instinct for a timecard. We could transform
their paycheck, like a dove
out of a magician's hat,
into grief. We could hurt, open that hole
in the center of our chests– I mean
the universe–
and jump right in.

TIKKUN ḤATZOT

I ask my mother if she knows
our ancestral tradition has a prayer service
you can do alone, where you wake up

in the middle of the night
and sit on the floor
and cry.

She says it's great
to get credit
for something

we're all doing anyway.

DIASPORA BLESSING FOR MULTIPLE NEW YEARS

Blessed are you for bending time,
future-traveler, moving within
your neighbor's last year
while in your new year.

//

Blessed is your witness
to the lunar seasons
dancing in the background
of calendars.

//

Blessed is your shapeshifting
of your moon-cycled body
into more rigid months,
and your balancing of spells,
calling each by their names.

//

Blessed are you, shadow traveler, blessing candles
to honor your day while inside their nights,
beginning your day before
the world you move within is ready.

//

Blessed are you, disassimilationist, who lives
among another's time and retains your own
entirely. Blessed also are you,
brave traveler, who moves
between worlds.

MY NAME

belonged to my great-
grandmother. I am only
carrying it.

ON THE LAST DAY OF PASSOVER

We studied Torah.
Per her birthday request,
we rested as our friend blessed us
with every word of Noach from memory, a tradition
lost for over a thousand years.
We shook our hips
to her promise of holy rainbows
in the lilt of her Moroccan grandfather.
We built her an ark
the way the world was created:
with words. We put on it
what we wanted for her in her coming year:
love and queer dance parties. Dayenu.
Those of us who had heard the news
of the latest shooting
decided not to tell those who hadn't,
who had led their phones to rest,
letting Shabbat breathe
the way she was intended.
When the sun was done with us for this day,
we walked together, made a circle
in the park, held the softness of spices safe
inside the sanctuary of their scarf,
smelled the smells of their sweet scent.
We lit up havdalah candles twisted up in each other.
We waved goodbye to Pesach.
In darkness, in public, we welcomed the week.
We separated day from night, celebrated our difference.
In place of distinguishing
our people from other nations,
we praised the necessity of coexistence—
to build a new world through them, called out
alone and together, comfort and challenge,
hope and satisfaction. We opened
the windows of ourselves, sent the night out searching
for our collective liberation like a raven
for the end of the flood. We offered our glittering selves on the altar.
We were remembered and we remembered.

On the other side of the garden, new
strangers
in this strange land
could hear us sing.

NOTES

This poem responded to the shooting that occurred on Passover at the Chabad of Poway synagogue.

THE WHOLE STORY

In her kitchen wallpapered in violets,
my grandmother warns me to love
everyone, to never hate

anyone's skin, tradition or country –
not after the decimation that found her family.

To know that *other* marks the beginning of death,
to know this separation transforms us humans into
the murderers and the murdered in minutes.

This is the way I learn to love,
begin to carry an open heart
caged in bones soaked in terror.

I will spend years renaming the plot—
love because love is who you are.
That's it. That's the whole story.

SETTLING UP

After Rembrandt, Self-Portrait, 1659

I wanted beautiful things: to hold the earth-
enware and smell its coffee beans, your face
in the morning soft before waking, the latest new
moon covert and still loved. I wanted
couture too. I wanted god-
et hemlines with fairytale endings, frothy
tulle sleeves, purses
in ice blues and cherry reds
with gold chains to grasp
and swing. I wanted to chase a life
in the world
that felt a little
like a romantic comedy on a movie theater screen:
big and ordinary and out of reach,
and come home to a life of aging
Rembrandt's self-portrait: the sunlight
revealing our rumpled faces,
our willingness
to hold on to the shadows.

AFTER THE ROBBERY

Oh. You didn't know? Your home
is a body. Let the walls shake, they are
managing too. Let your floors reverberate
with memory.

When you replay the night in your mind,
let them come in.
While you are sleeping.
As they did.

This, this thieving,
where you did not leave your bed
to tell them to get out.
Say thank G-d. This thieving
where nobody dies—

Let it happen
as it happened,
sleeping beside sweet love.
You, soft,
as you have waited your whole life
to become.

THE MERCY SEAT

In between its wings,
the goldcrest kinglet is made
of such fragile bones.

CONTROL

In this version of the story, when he hands
me a book on women who cannot give up
control, I hand it back. I tell him this book
is an attempt to control me.

The therapist does not ask when I will cease gripping
onto myself like I am holding together pieces
of a broken vase, filled
with the last taste of water
for a thirsty mouth. Neither

does the lover. They each hold
their tongues, literally: their tongues slither
out of their mouths into one hundred eels.
Two hands are not enough to hold
back so many eels.

In this version of the story,
when their accusations wriggle
out, I don't throw myself
in after, tossing myself into
this current. I do not need
to be a metaphor every time.

In this version of the story, I say, *Yeah, I like control. So what?*

I have been enough metaphors. Here's one:

Out of control meant I was a car and you were the wheel
and I don't surrender to small gods anymore.

In this version of the story, nobody says, *Surrender.*

I ask myself the questions, like
*Has your own body been a game
you were not invited to play?*

In this version of the story, nobody asks when I will give up control.

In this version of the story,
I am safe.

SWIM

after Li-Young Lee

A body is three-fourths winter
and the rest a hot summer rain.
Forget what you know
about corporeal water
for just this moment.

A body's one-part frozen lake in a rural town,
the area ominous
when you aren't familiar, thrilling
to find, and to be, this almost-smooth, uneven
dance floor, temporary and precarious.

Water holds
memory of where
it has been. When this ice cracks,
the rift warns
I will be unburdened
of beliefs.

//

We have been fighting
all week and making love to come
up for air from drowning. Every
morning we promise
each other we will work
this out, but we haven't touched
entirely what *this* is. Each word we throw
out threatens a proof that may disintegrate
the other's thesis of Self. Say it
in ice: Once, we drew
our names in a heart
into the rime, recognizing
its potential for melting.

A body lives
in layers of ice and bone
and tropical storm. Tell me you're here
on purpose, tell me you didn't just press
your lips to my frost
and get stuck here.

Stumbling over fissures in our brittle
identities, our hoarded traumas bubble
up through the lake's melting
surface we are sure
will break us open and bury
us alive under water. Witness, this slab
of frozen personas splitting,
I believe could drown us, signals
spring is blooming. If I can navigate
the map of this shattering,
I may yet
swim.

A HOWLING WILDERNESS

and in chaos, a howling wildernness
(Devarim 32:10)

I scored ninety percent
on the C-PTSD quiz. I had waited
for the counselor to review and reveal I didn't
have the symptoms. She had to tell me
90 percent is a lot of trauma to be carrying.

Who taught us
to accept so much
as so little
and so little
as enough?

When I was born, I was around
seventy percent water,
like my mother,
Earth.

I am ninety percent trauma
on the intake quiz.

Lately, I have a mind like a sieve.
It holds the void, the badlands,
and lets the glimmers of lush
hope fall through. I have a mind
like a sieve, but not in the way
I thought it would work.

What if I told you this lost, this crawl
through the murky fog,
is not a waste? You will grieve in it,
you will claw for something
to drag you out of here, and that thing will be
in you, it will have been passed on

from desolation to desolation,
and then from inside this howling wilderness,
you will heal.

RECKONING

You have to know you're enough.
And you have to remember.
Then,
        you have to
                forget
and tumble into the soft darkness
and let it hold you
Sometimes,
             if you're lucky
it will whisper
        to you
          secrets:
              like,
        this is happening
        you are alive
              (even if)
              (just barely)
        and when you are on the edge of mercy
        in that pillow embrace
              of that god
              that you have called pain
        you have to let it toss you
        back into the earthen world
        and lay you on its ground
        until you say
              I do
              I want to be here
        and   this   time
I mean it.

TEHILLAH

let me be a drop of spit
in Your mouth
so that when you speak,
i taste a lick
of creating the universe.

ITINERANT

You're driving south on Farm to Market Road 243. The sun follows
on your right. The nighthawk, its black wings sporting white bands,

mourns in reverse. You round the curve of road
and the sun abandons you. To be human is to superimpose

yourself over everything. You feel the warmth again touch
your shoulder and curl up in your mother's rocking arms. The mock-
ingbird

rushes home over tin houses and hay bails, over a meadow held in a
single belt
of rusted barbed wire, above the Mahomet Christian Church, past

the arched sign for Mahomet Cemetery. A body
of cedar elms guards her buried children from view.

There is so much to believe
is speaking.

It's the *to you* which brings loneliness—
as if something is happening only to you,

as if something is not
always happening.

SHE'ELAT ḤALOM

she'elat ḥalom שאלת חלום – *literally "dream question,"*
a practice of finding answers through dreaming

These were the signs
of my dreams: the wooden table
and the wooden chair
rough-hewn from the weathered spiral trunk
of a lodgepole pine, 3 grains of rice—
3 grains of grace, the voice was saying—
the burlap sack in which to carry them
(the coarse body,
the bumpy life), the outrage a hot coal
in my chest in which to burn or boil
the harvested seed, all of it, comes down
to these: they are: 3 grains
of rice, sustenance, 3 grains of grace,
enough.

EIGHT PHASES OF RECREATING THE WORLD

After Wallace Stevens

I.

A crater is a wound,
gaping evidence of violence.

II.

The crater's empty space
shoulders a keepsake
that outlasts a flag.

III.

I and the crater
are one.
I and the wound
are one.
My body, the crater, and the wound
are one.

IV.

There are craters I want
to find tenements in,
and establish my life
in a tenuous atmosphere,
scientifically demonstrated,
instead of constantly wondering.

V.

Let me start over.
Permit me to begin again.
Allow me
to regenerate.

VI.

The outer skin regenerates
in cycles. At 40 years,
every 28 days, so I am no longer
in the same skin as when it happened.
His hand's skin, his body's skin
new also. He knew. Also.

VII.

Which cells are the same cells?
Which of the brain cells?
What will the soul sell to release itself?
How many times did I sell myself
short or for a meteoric soar in ransom,
trying to earn enough to buy myself
out of this body?

VIII.

I orbit my own earth.
You wouldn't know what to do
with these craters.

WHEN THEY SEE ME COMING,

tell them I am wolf.
Warn them I have become
more claw than thumb.
Let them know I sleep
fur pile with my family now.
When we travel, we are the route.
I rest soft-bellied against the earth—
on the forest floor, on rocks, in the desert.
When I see fanged jaws open
towards us, I prepare
to gnaw through bone.

JUST THIS

May I grow feral
and tender
and know when
for each

AFTER SHOCK

tremor *(n.) late 14c., "terror," from Old French tremor "fear, terror, quaking" (13c.), from Latin tremorem "a trembling, terror." (- Online Etymology Dictionary)*

This is how trauma lives in the body
as the rumble and sting within skin:
it is fed with doubt. We feed it disbelief,
without ever asking what it hungers for, for soothing,
and the trauma begins to tremble.

After shock, there is always shaking.
After the earth's tremor and quake, a fear of the earth.
But the land needs soothing
and so do its people. Communities gather, share stories,
bring each other meals, begin to rebuild
houses where houses can be built. After an earthquake,
nobody tells us it didn't happen. After the ground opens,
no one ever threatens you for mentioning it.

When you turn your head away from your story
while it whispers to you, it rocks itself against your body
still murmuring, inside the living room with no ceiling, walls blown out,
where you insist the quake wasn't that strong.

This is how trauma lives in the body
as a buzzing, an electric spasm against the spine:
you tell yourself others have it worse (and they do,
and so what?), you tell yourself it wasn't that bad,
you tell yourself you can't let your story speak.
If you have turned from your story, if you are wary of
everyone you meet, go easy on yourself. This is trauma
doing what it was designed, when fed disbelief, to do. If you are waiting
to tell of what happened
in a way that frees your breath and,
no matter who you tell, no matter who believes you,
you still feel the aftermath tremor shaking inside your exposed skin,
consider this: hold yourself tight and say: *I believe you.*

I believe you.
It happened
exactly
as you say.

WALLPAPER FROM THE WALLS OF THE HEALING ROOM

YOU,

as open canon— a
continuous and fluid,
believed revelation.

You,

as you are,

as the prophetic answer
our wildest imagination
could not have dreamed.

//

autobiography of all of us:

we are healers. and.
we are healing.

//

in this version
of the story,
you remember you are whole.

//

you have called yourself
so many terrible things. call yourself
a blessing

//

I love you, world,
even though you
break my heart
every day. And
I'm wagering I
break yours.

//

i am made
from the mystery
and the mystery
is in me —
my action is my prayer.

//

like ancient
ruins, I am
ancient. ruin.
what survives
can be visited.
send your
archeologists. i am
living proof.

THE FATES

When I am born and washed,
my mother

hands me over
to my grandfather. He cradles

his firstborn
grandchild, peers into her midnight

cavernous eyes
and acquaints her:

Life is hard
and people are difficult.

The new parents implore
the old patriarch's name– *Bill!*– disrupting

a curse. The young father, amateur
to fatherhood, seizes

his infant back, her nakedness
falling

out of her swaddling,
and returns

baby to mother's arms. Maybe
it was too late. Or, perhaps

each of the trio spoke their dialogue
and danced their choreography

on cue, a play of the fates
weaving

a world. Now, I know
my grandfather was right

and also,
that he was not.

WONDER

We know the sun doesn't rise
anymore or set. And yet we're determined
to continue this myth. We gather on beaches,
light bonfires. Some people clap
to see that glowing orb go down. Our rituals
and traditions. We know. We know the water isn't the end of it all.
We know we're not the only planet that exists,
that the universe extends past the horizon.
That the sun doesn't really sink down into the underworld
below us and wake up the next day, rallying us too to begin.
We know this. We have known for years.
And yet we remain committed
to the celebration of this story. To believe what we also know isn't true.
I hope, one day, they write about us. How confusing we were,
and charming. How we lived in that liminal space,
when we had been told
that we were turning, turning, turning
around the nearest star. That there was no such thing
as a sunrise or a sunset. And knowing this completely,
we still chose to believe.

REPAIRING MIDNIGHT

Night and I are familiar beasts,
we have been tender wild things.
In this fair shake, we agree
to give it a go among the starlight:
all the lost causes twinkling
down on us, just like us,
long finished
and still shining.

SHELTER PUP

He wriggles under my blanket and stretches
his paw out onto my hand
to remind me I am still animal. He whimpers
and burrows into my arms, then growls
at the thundering sky. The lightning

is an LED grid, the thunder— a deep
house beat. I watch the nervous and flaunting
clouds, having crammed all the rain they could
into their tight dresses, wait
urgently on the line to be allowed in
to burst. Tonight,

I am chamomile tea. I am a collection
of poetry from the library. Against
my better judgment, I let this pup,
new from the shelter, stay in the bed
one more night, because I remember

what it is to be lost,
and then found by a family you make,
to snarl at everything
when you are terrified,
to need a bouncer
to nod towards you
and let you in
from the cold.

IN THE DROUGHT

We were afraid of everything
but not as much
as everything was afraid of us. After
they inhaled our lungs passing by, the trees breathed
back to us their terror. We divided the world

by species, then divided species
by who was us, then divided us by
who was them. Who wasn't us we wanted
dead.

But everyone is us. We are in
everything. We will not die.
We keep coming back,
like rain.

SEGULAH FOR THE AFTERMATH

I inscribed inside my amulet
body. I recited it at home
and on my way, when I lay down,
and as I got up. I wrapped it
between my fingers, wore its chant
as a crown, bound it around
my forehead as a jewel
between my eyes to ward off
any evil eye from staring
back and causing
me to doubt. I nailed
it to the doorposts of my skin
and kissed my fingers to it,
emblazoned this into each gate
I approached and passed through
and it has protected me each day:
You are strong enough
to take the sum of your experiences
and make something wonderful
and it has kept me alive, sustained me,
and brought me to this season.

HOPE

hope stopped coming home here
and I don't know how to tell her
she is welcome.
she reminds me
in a love letter
that she is not magic.
there are no special words
to make her appear. but I can say,
thank you.
for everything you've done so far.
and she will know
to start
heading home.

HOW TO HEAL AND WRITE AT THE SAME TIME

Write about yourself
like you would anyone
you've had the privilege to awe. Write
about how meeting
you was a miracle. How you were
so full of and bursting with a boundless
mystery. How you bubbled
with a sacred unknown. How you couldn't
begin to claim
to know all of your being. How you were
grateful to get to listen.
To be a witness
to the testimony of your existence.
Start there.

TAKING IN VAIN CAN ALSO BE TRANSLATED AS BEARING EMPTINESS

Language, I wanted to be your humble servant. I gave
myself away to so many smaller gods.

And I bore emptiness, didn't I? And emptiness
is the heaviest to bear. Even the good kind,

unwieldy to grasp. I could caress
something warm and sweet and vast

and let it fill me. Isn't every whisper and mumble
a stumbled prayer, a request, a bid for a return home, or bathing

our hands in appreciation? If eating without blessing
equates theft, could blessing be currency

in the coming world and if that world is always arriving,
could we start right now?

Baruch shem kevod malchuto l'olam va'ed.

TKHINE

May I be my fire offering.
May I bring
my life,
the most delicious
panting offering
I can bring
and stomach
annihilating in fire.

BLESSING FOR DIASPORA AS A SPIRITUAL PRACTICE

To be alive
is to attend a prayer service.
To do the work of the heart
in the temple of the world,
to build
the tender center of that temple
inside yourself,
is a blessing:
to seek for that center again and again
in everyone, each body a tent for conducting
its own ceremony into ascension,
to build the altar within you
and decide what you will sacrifice
and who you will not,
to hold all the brokenness
for the sake of any chance of repair,
to welcome everyone exiled,
everything broken
from its origins,
all holiness ripped
from its dwelling places,
and chant together,
here, here, here.

B'REISHIT BEDTIME STORY

blessed is the one who spoke
and the world came to be
- Jewish Blessing

The songs were starfish
when the Oneness spoke. A sound split
off into a moon, another calling
out became a wheat field.
And the voice regrew, and broke
off into our ancestors
and they, severed,
regenerated and we, all, remain
swimming out here, fragments
of the First
and Endless
vibrating breath.

THE SHAPE OF OURSELVES

My neighbor wants to know
how I'm doing, so I show him
the wooden altar I'm building that holds
the weight of a person

and he says, *Whoah, that's some heavy*
Abraham and Isaac business,
and sure, but not everything
weighs as much

as those two. I wanted a place
for us all to sit
and consider
how much we have to offer,

which doesn't carry
the heft of sacrificing
your child, but has
consequence.

I wanted a scripture that whispers, *I am the world,*
and you too are the world,
and the repairing of this world
is more of a remembering. I wanted
a hymn that sings, *We are made in the likeness*
of all that is holy— and in the likeness
of each other.

We will shape ourselves
into the shape of ourselves,
in this lifetime,
I swear.

GLOSSARY

An introduction to some of the non-English words in this collection. Each of these words could be a book. These are a summary. Hebrew letters do not include capitals. Lowercase transliterations provided below reflect that.

ayeka (Hebrew: איכה): "Where are you?" The first question G-d asks of a person in Torah, the first divine call to *Adam/ adam* (B'resheit 3:9).

bamidbar (Hebrew: במדבר): "In the Wilderness," "In the Desert" (*ba*: "in"; *midbar*: "wilderness," "desert"). The name of the book in Torah known in English as The Book of Numbers, *Bamidbar* is also the name of the Torah portion in this book, which includes the census and the priests' duties.

b'resheit (Hebrew: בראשית): Literally, "In the Beginning." The first book, portion, and word of the Torah: the book translated as Genesis; the first weekly Torah portion in the yearly Jewish cycle of reading the Torah.

emunah (Hebrew: אמונה): Loose translation, "faith."

ḥai (Hebrew: חי) (Often transliterated *chai* with a guttural "ch"): "living," "alive." The letters חי are also used as a symbol, for life.

niggun (Hebrew: ניגון): "melody," "tune." Also refers to a form of Jewish religious song or tune, usually with repetitive sounds such as "Lai-Lai-Lai", instead of formal lyrics.

segulah (Hebrew: סגולה): Multiple meanings, such as "treasure," and "heirloom;" in this context "remedy" or "protection."

shanah me'uberet (Hebrew: שנה מעוברת) Also spelled *shanah me'uberes* (Ashkenaz): Literally "pregnant year," refers to a year with a thirteenth moon/ moon cycle/ month.

tehillah (Hebrew: תהלה): "praise," "psalm."

tkhine (Yiddish: תחינה from the Hebrew *tachanun* תחנון): "plea," "supplication." Tkhines especially refer to Yiddish prayers and devotions, and collections of these, written from a woman's personal viewpoint, for women, particularly popular from the 1600s to the early 1800s.

tikkun ḥatzot (Hebrew: תקון חצות) Also spelled *tikkun chatzos* (Ashkenaz): "Midnight Rectification," a Jewish mystic ritual prayer recited in the middle of the night.

tzadik (Hebrew: צדיק): "righteous [one]," a Jewish title given to those considered righteous, such as figures in Torah or a great spiritual leader and teacher of a generation.

ADDITIONAL NOTES

*p.26 gevurah-din/ chesed/ tifere*t are arranged to the Sephirot, the Divine Emanations.

p.32 "may this be an action/ of healing, for You heal/ without charge" is from a traditional Jewish blessing in Hebrew. In English, it loosely translates as "May it be Your will, Hashem, my G-d, that this enterprise [or action] will be for me for a healing (and some add, "because You are a Healer who heals freely/ without payment") (Babylonian Talmud Brachot 60a, Shulchan Aruch 230:4 and Mishna Berurah 6).

p.36 "How great is Your emunah" (Hebrew: רבה אמונתך, transliteration: *rabbah emunatecha*): "How great is Your faith," is from the *Modeh Ani* morning prayer.

p.71 "has kept me alive, sustained me, and brought me to this season" is from the *Shehecheyanu* blessing: "who has kept us alive, sustained us, and brought us to this season."

p.74 Baruch shem kevod malchuto l'olam va'ed (Hebrew: ברוך שם כבוד מלכותו לעולם ועד): Said in multiple contexts, including in daily prayers, a person also says this to rectify having inadvertently said G-d's name in vain and render the utterance acceptable– for example, accidentally reciting an incorrect blessing (the formula for blessing includes the name), so that one will not be considered to have recited a blessing in vain (Maimonedes, *Mishneh Torah*, Blessings 4:10).

ACKNOWLEDGMENTS

I am grateful for the editors and curators of the following publications and venues, in which versions of these poems appeared: Rattle ("On the Last Day of Passover"); The Los Angeles Press ("Swim," "The Romanian Jew Flees To The U.S. For A Better Life But All Her Granddaughter Dreams Of Is Wailing," "Segulah For The Aftermath," "The Offering," "Wonder"); The Ekphrastic Review ("Settling Up"); Ritualwell ("How to Bless Yourself," "Blessing for Diaspora as a Spiritual Practice," "On the Last Day of Passover"); Life as Ceremony ("Diaspora Prayer Of The Refugee's Grandchild"); Hevria Magazine ("Rough Bark"); F(Empower) Magazine ("After the Robbery").

"Hymn To Bloodletting, Sacrifice of Becoming" first appeared as a recording for Radio Bloomsday, directed by Caraid O'Brien.

"Wallpaper from the Walls of the Healing Room" first appeared as the series of panels, "Call Yourself a Blessing" in The Healing Room of the Alena Museum, Oakland, CA, curated by Adrian Bello, Alliance Den.

"The Shape of Ourselves" was written for, and first performed at, *We Put Our Bodies On the Altar*, an interactive installation, performance art, and show based on my poems, for the *Reflections on Exile* exhibit at Root Division Gallery, San Francisco, CA, curated by Jeannette Alanis.

All names that refer to someone real who are not family members have been changed.